PRESBYTERIAN PRINCIPLES.

A DISCOURSE

Delivered in the Jefferson Park Church, Chicago, on Sabbath, Feb. 1st, 1875.

— BY —

FRANCIS L. PATTON, D. D.

CHICAGO:
METROPOLITAN PRINTING CO., 90 & 92 FIFTH AVE.

1875.

CHICAGO, April 2d, 1875.

REV. FRANCIS L. PATTON, D. D.,

DEAR SIR :

Having read with great satisfaction your sermon on the Principles, Polity, &c., of the Presbyterian Church, published in a recent number of THE INTERIOR, and believing that a more extended circulation of this discourse will do more to remove misapprehensions existing in the minds of many persons in regard to the teachings and views of our beloved church, and possibly induce them to seek a home in our household of faith, we respectfully and earnestly request your consent to its publication in Tract form.

Very sincerely yours,

C. B. NELSON,
E. S. WELLS,
JOHN V. FARWELL,
H. G. MILLER.

CHICAGO, April 19th, 1875.

GENTLEMEN:

I thank you for your kind words respecting my sermon on "Presbyterian Principles," and herewith send you a corrected copy, in accordance with the request contained in your letter of 2d instant.

Very sincerely yours,

FRANCIS L. PATTON.

To Messrs. C. B. NELSON, E. S. WELLS,
JOHN V. FARWELL, and H. G. MILLER.

PRESBYTERIAN PRINCIPLES.

"The laying on of the hands of the presbytery."—1 Timothy, iv., 14.

I invite attention to the principles which underlie our form of government. Nor is the discussion upon which I enter altogether unneeded. For it would be a great mistake to suppose that all who worship in Presbyterian churches are *ex animo* Presbyterians. And I do not make the remark in any disparaging sense either, I would have you understand. A great many circumstances occur to take people inside the Presbyterian Church. Some, to be sure, are born in it, as most of us were; some come in by marriage; some make a home in it because they do not find any church which would exactly correspond with their ecclesiastical preferences, though this may come nearest to such a correspondence. This is all right. And so we, to-day, for one cause or another, find ourselves ecclesiastically related to the Shorter Catechism and the Westminster Confession of Faith. There can be no harm, then, in our knowing exactly what is meant by being a Presbyterian. I do not wish to be regarded to-day as blowing the trumpet of sectarianism. A minister may be about better business. But it is possible to show the reason for our preferences as members of a particular church without saying anything to the discredit of other churches, just as it is possible for us to seek to build up our own congregation without grudging our neighbor the ground he occupies.

The peculiarities of the Presbyterian denomination are found in two things; its polity and its creed. It is in regard to its polity that I intend to speak particularly.

I. POLITY.

On the general question of church polity there are three leading views. There are those who believe in the principle of individualism. They do not believe in the divine authority, or in the practical value of a church organization and a standing ministry. There are some good Christian people, earnest, devout, and enthusiastic in their attachment to the doctrines of grace, of whom it is nevertheless true that their influence is disintegrating, and that it would be destructive of the church's organic life were it to hold sway. Next to the sacerdotalism which unchurches all who do not belong to a prelatic communion do we deprecate the individualism which would disorganize the Church by disparaging the ordained ministry. Our feelings of regret and our sense of the wrong which is done in both cases are not lessened by the consciousness that some of the most devout and devoted of God's servants are found in both classes. There are those again who hold the expediential view of church polity. They maintain that as great enterprises can be most wisely undertaken by joint action, so the work of Christians can be best performed in a corporate capacity. If we wish to build expensive railroads, we must put the funds of individuals in a joint stock. If we wish to make aggressive war, it is necessary to muster an army and put it under efficient command. So if we are to do the work which Christ has left his disciples to perform, there must be an understanding among us and concerted action. Moreover, as the same man cannot do one thing well if he has everything to do, it is proper that there should be a class of men who will hold themselves responsible for ministering in word and doctrine. The minister, they maintain, is evolved by the law of division of labor, the same as the lawyer and the physician.

This is as far as some are willing to go. And since they found their doctrine of the need of a polity upon expediency, of course they will not be particular about the form which that polity assumes, though their preference may incline them to one rather than another. They say:

> "For forms of government let fools contest,
> That which is best administered is best."

In all our churches men of this sort are to be found. And there are, thirdly, those who believe in a *jure divino* system of polity. That is to say, they believe that at least the outlines of an ecclesiastical polity are laid down in the New Testament, and that New Testament precedent is to be our guide in the organization of the church. The Episcopal, the Presbyterian, and the Congregational churches are all based upon the *jure divino* idea, and represent the three different opinions in regard to what the New Testament polity is.

Now the Presbyterian polity is summed up in three cardinal principles: 1 Parity of the Ministry. 2. Popular Government. 3. Ecclesiastical Unity. Let us notice these in their order.

1. Parity of the Ministry.

We believe that all ministers of Christ are on the same level. And this marks the point of our divergence from Episcopalians. The latter say that there are three orders of ministers: deacons, priests and bishops. We say there is only one order; that deacons are not ministers, but laymen; that the word priest is an abbreviated expression for presbyter; and that presbyter and bishop are two words for the same office. There was a time when the Episcopal office was defended by an appeal to the passages in which Paul speaks of bishops. But biblical interpretation was in its youth then. No scholar would risk his reputation by any such appeal nowadays. The old argument is fairly on the shelf, inasmuch as nothing is more certain than that Paul calls the same men in Acts xx. both elders and bishops. Because it is common for us to speak of ministers as pastors, it does not follow that pastors and ministers are two distinct classes of men. The usual mode of arguing now, is to assume that the three orders originally were apostles, presbyters and deacons; that bishops are successors of the apostles, though out of reverence for the original twelve their successors are not called by this name. And no fault can be found with this argument except that it is gratuitous. There is no evidence that the apostolic office was meant to be perpetual, and there is no reason why the name should not be continued if the office was. The best testimony to the substantial accuracy of the position taken here comes from a man of undoubted scholarship and of high position in the university of Cambridge, England. Prof. Lightfoot concedes the whole argument which Presbyterians are in the habit of making, and defends Episcopacy on the strength of antiquity. Its charter, he virtually says, is not in the New Testament, but Episcopacy grew up so early that it may fairly claim to have apostolic sanction. It is enough for us, however, that its charter is not in the New Testament. The argument from antiquity is worth very little, and a man needs more than mortal vision to see through the fog of patristic literature so as to discern the outlines of the ecclesiastical polity of the apostolic age. Now, the differences and the alienations which keep Presbyterians and Episcopalians apart grow out of their denial of our principle of parity of the ministry, or, if that is the more complimentary way of putting it, our denial of their principle that there are three orders in the ministry. Bishops are higher in rank than presbyters or priests. Bishops alone can confirm, can ordain. A church without ordination is a church without a ministry. But a church without a ministry is not a church at all. Hence, Presbyterians have no church, for they have no ministry; for they have no ordination; for they have no bishop.

High Church Episcopacy is open to serious objections. It lays grievous burdens upon its advocates. But it is consistent. If we held High Church premisses, we should hold High Church conclusions, too. We have great respect for the learning, piety and devotion of high church leaders. But *apostolic succession* is the *proton pseudos* of the system. It is well that the Reformed Episcopalians have rejected the dogma. Had they retained it they would have made shipwreck of their cause, and their separation from the "Protestant Episcopal church" would have been uncalled for.

The parity of the ministry, then, is our first principle. All ministers are on a level. The young man has as good a right to vote as the old man. Neither gray hairs, nor a doctorate in divinity, nor a large salary, nor a metropolitan pulpit, gives any man a place an inch above the young man, the untitled man, or the minister of a rural charge. I do not mean that every man's opinion has the same weight. Men differ in brains, in industry, in spiritual power, in ripeness of experience, in their competency to speak upon and deal with different subjects, and it is right that these elements should be taken into account in the respect which is accorded to them. But there is no official superiority recognized in the Presbyterian church.

2. Popular Government. We believe that the people have a right to be

heard in the management of the church's affairs. Everything which concerns the management of the church's spiritual affairs is, on Presbyterian principles, the joint action of the ministers and the people. We are not always understood in this respect. By our Congregational brethren our system is sometimes looked upon as a hierarchy. Now, the difference between us and our Congregational brethren in this respect, grows mainly out of the third principle, which I shall announce presently. The people have a right to be heard. Presbyterians say this as strongly as Congregationalists. The difference between us is in regard to the question, How shall they be heard? Directly, or by representatives? Shall these parties be received into membership? Shall these be dismissed? Is this man accused of wrong deserving of censure, or is he not? Shall we sing as a congregation or by proxy? All these are questions on which the people have a right to an opinion. Only in the Presbyterian church they express it by their representatives, the Elders.

The representative system which we have adopted provides for the expression of the popular will. A Congregational church might elect and ordain Elders and commit the management of its affairs to them without destroying its Congregational character. The elders of a Presbyterian church are the representatives of the people, appointed by them to act for them in the management of their spiritual interests. That is a simple matter. Says our Form of Government, chapter v.: "Ruling elders are properly the representatives of the people, chosen by them for the purpose of exercising government and discipline in conjunction with pastors or ministers."

In our church we set great store by the eldership. To their prudence, piety and wisdom, the church, under God, owes, in very great degree, her peace, purity and prosperity. They are men upon whom the minister can rely for cool judgment, sound advice, and hearty co-operation; and he is a foolish minister who goes outside the circle of the session for counsel, or who seeks to act independently of his constitutional advisers. In these days, when the pastoral office is generally of brief and always of uncertain tenure, the eldership should become even more important. The elders are permanent. Their families belong to the church. They have an interest not only in the cause of Christ generally, but in the cause of Christ as promoted by the particular church of which they are members. Congregations would do well to be jealous of the honor due to the elders, and on no account should the eldership be treated as an office co-ordinately related to the trusteeship, as it sometimes is. It would add greatly we believe to the efficiency of our church, as well as to the comfort and success of her ministers, if throughout our land the sessions were willing to assume or free to exercise to the full the duties of their office. But if this were done at once it would be a revolution.

3. Ecclesiastical Unity. The only debatable ground on the subject of church polity, lies, in my judgment, between Presbyterianism and Congregationalism. Prelacy has not a leg to stand upon,—scripturally. I do not say that the Episcopal form of government has no excellencies, or that men have no right to adopt it. What I do say is that a ministry of three orders cannot be found in the New Testament. The only battle is between Congregationalists and Presbyterians. And the real difference between Congregationalists and Presbyterians lies in the meaning of the word church. The idea and the error of Congregationalism is the doctrine of absolute congregational independence.

Out and out Congregationalism is not the prevailing system in this country among the Congregational churches. But the principle of Congregational polity is that every congregation is independent. It can manage its own affairs; elect, ordain, install and dismiss its pastors as it pleases; try, acquit, censure, excommunicate offenders beyond hope of redress; split, combine, swarm, multiply as convenience or selfishness may suggest. Congregationalism of this radical type is not the prevailing form of Congregational polity in this land. Generally the different Congregational Churches own a relationship to each other; the smaller recognize the moral weight of the larger bodies, and though a Congregational council has only advisory power, its decisions nevertheless receive serious consideration. In a word, and we say it in no exultant tone, Congregationalism has been more or less Presbyterianized, as in fact Presbyterianism may have been to some extent Congregationalized.

It would be easy to occupy time in the citations of texts and arguments in defence of the positions taken in this sermon, but I shall do so only to a limited extent. The issue between Congregationalists and Presbyterians as to the breadth of the word *church* can only be settled by an examination of the passages in the New Testament in which the word occurs. Presbyterians are accustomed to argue, and it seems to me with a great deal of force, that the application of the word to denote the Christians living in a city, is proof that its meaning is not confined to those who worship statedly under the same roof. For example, Paul does not speak of the *churches* of Ephesus, but of the *church* of Ephesus. On the Congregational theory, therefore, we are bound to believe that after Paul had been preaching three years in that large city, there was only a handful of converts who could get inside the walls of an ordinary dwelling for stated worship. For you must remember that was before the day of large churches, it was in fact at a time when church-going would not have been the safest thing in the world either. Similarly with the church of Jerusalem — church, mark, not churches, though three thousand people were converted in one day, and that was before the day of "tabernacles." I might cite other examples, but these are sufficient to show that the word "church" is not a synonym for congregation. Indeed a leading Congregationalist divine in England, Dr. Stoughton, has conceded as much in his able essay on "The Primitive Ecclesia." His view is that all Christians living within the bounds of a municipality ought to be embraced under the word church. As if all the Christians in Chicago were known as the Church of Chicago, and were absolutely independent of churches outside the corporate limits of our city. This view is to be sure not Presbyterian, but it is fatal to Congregationalism. The moment the principle is accepted that all the congregations in a city are or may be under corporate jurisdiction the absolute character of Congregationalism has passed away. The difference between us and our Congregational brethren in the interpretation of the word *ecclesia* makes the difference in the two systems of ecclesiastical polity which are so apparent. With them, each congregation manages its own affairs, calls whom it pleases and retains his services as long as it pleases. It gives no account to any higher judicatory of its actions, and has no tribunal of an authoritative kind before whom the aggrieved can appear. Our view of the matter entails upon us a great deal of machinery and restrains our liberty. We are not as independent as Congregationalists are. We are not so irresponsible. The question is whether this loss of liberty is made up by counter-balancing advantages. We cannot install a pastor without the concurrence of Presbytery. We cannot dissolve the pastoral relation without its sanction. Nay, we neither form it nor dissolve it. Presbytery does both. Of course the great reason which we have for advocating Presbyterianism is that it is scriptural. We believe in the divine right of Presbytery. But there are obvious advantages connected with our system of polity.

1. It protects the church against unreasonable divisions. In the Congrega-

tional system a church may colonize just when it pleases. When men are offended, or not suited, the most ready way of settling the difficulty is to build a new church under the eaves of the old one, to be an eye-sore to the minister and people of the old congregation. "That is the beauty of our system," say the Congregationalists. But that depends very much upon your point of view. It is a very simple matter of arithmetic to show that a given number of people who can barely support one pastor are unequal to the task of supporting two, when supporting two means erecting another edifice, paying two sextons, two gas bills, two fuel bills, two organists, and sometimes two choirs, for churches usually get ambitious under these circumstances. Now the system which allows the undue multiplication of churches is an unjust one. When a congregation becomes large enough to divide without injury to the pastor, it is right enough to do so; but until it does, division is unkind, and unkind because it puts a yoke of care around the neck of a man who has care enough without the additional anxiety of asking, "What shall I eat, what shall I drink, and wherewithal shall I be clothed?" That is why I like the Presbyterian system. It can say to those who contemplate a new enterprise: "No, there is no room for another church in your town. You are unable to do justice to one pastor, and it is folly for you to attempt the support of two."

2. Another advantage of our system is, that it gives opportunity to every man of having justice done him. We have a gradation of courts. First, the Session, composed of the minister and the ruling elders; then the Presbytery, composed of all the ministers of a district, and an elder from each congregation; then the Synod, composed of a number of presbyteries; and then the General Assembly, which is a representative body made up of commissioners from all the Presbyteries of our church. Every decision of an inferior adjudicatory may

come before the higher courts in one of four ways: by appeal, complaint, reference, and review, and control. If a man is unjustly dealt with in the Session, he can be heard in Presbytery; if dissatisfied with the action of Presbytery, he can appeal to Synod; if the Synod will not sustain him, he can appeal to the General Assembly, and by that time, if the judgment is still adverse, he should be ready to admit that he is wrong, or to bear his grievance in silence.

3. Our system makes provision for doctrinal purity on the part of its ministers. Nothing is said against the character of a man if it is affirmed that his theological views are unsound. Men differ materially in regard to what soundness is. Now the Presbyterian Church has a creed. All her ministers profess adherence to it. All Christians would not make a creed just like ours. We know as a matter of fact they do not. And we do not think the less of them as Christians for that either. But our church has a creed, and along with the great verities in which all Christians agree, are to be found the doctrines which are peculiar to us, and which justify our denominational existence. Our form of government is constructed on the supposition that men are not only free but "mutable." It contemplates the possibility that men will depart from the faith, and it provides a constitutional way whereby an exercise of an individual's right to change his belief may not imperil the doctrinal purity of the Church.

4. It will appear to anyone studying our system, how compact and symmetrical it is; how completely it answers the ends of popular government with such wise centralization of authority as is necessary to make any government efficient. In every matter which affects the interests of the Church, the people have a voice, and act through their representatives. This popular element goes into every department of the Presbyterian system. Ministers and elders sit together in every court, consult in every committee, and in the session the popular ele-

ment largely predominates. Yet the power is centralized. Take, for instance, the working of the affairs of a congregation. Everything in the management of a church, so far as worship is concerned, is in the hands of the session. Unnecessary questions are sometimes asked as to the extent of the session's jurisdiction. Some seem to favor the idea of putting some interests out of the session's reach, and of appointing extra committees to share the session's responsibilities. Some are disposed to regard the Sabbath-school as a separate institution. Some think the choir gallery is meant to hold another select committee, with powers which place them beyond sessional jurisdiction. Now the truth is, that the men whom the people elect to consult for the interest of the church, and who are solemnly set apart to the office of ruling elder, are the men who should manage the church's affairs. And to take any department of church work out of their hands and away from their jurisdiction is not only unpresbyterian, but is an indication of a want of respect for the ordained office bearers of the church. Everything pertaining to spiritual affairs that can in any way be made a matter of legislation belongs, according to our system, to the session. Whether members shall be received into or dismissed from a church; whether a certain mode of instruction shall be adopted in the Sabbath-school; whether the pastor shall superintend the school or a substitute, and if a substitute, whether he shall be appointed by the session or elected by the school; what collections for benevolent purposes shall be taken up; whether the church building shall be used for other than religious purposes; all these are questions of which the session has the right to take cognizance. And inasmuch as the people in all other matters speak through their representatives, it is of great importance that the right men should fill the office of ruling elder, and that when elected and ordained, they should have the respect and confidence of the congregation.

II. DOCTRINE.

Ministers and elders of the Presbyterian Church profess adherence in the Westminster Confession of Faith as containing the system of doctrine taught in the Word of God. It is a Calvinistic creed. We believe in predestination — the Trinity, the supreme divinity of Christ, total depravity, vicarious atonement, justification by faith, the eternal punishment of the impenitent, etc. Those who sit under Presbyterian preaching will hear these doctrines preached. While a man may reasonably be irritated when the minister does nothing but harp on one string, preaching God's justice as if He had no mercy, or speaking of the law as if there were no New Testamant, it is clearly unjust for him to be irritated at the infusion of doctrinal statement which a faithful and judicious minister will work into his sermons.

But the Confession of Faith subscribed to by ministers and elders is not understood to be subscribed to by private members. This leads me to some remarks on the idea of membership in the Presbyterian Church. Members of he visible church according to our standards are "believers and their children." Now suppose a case. A lady comes to me and says: "I would like to unite with your church, but have difficulty with some of the doctrines." I should say: Do you know that you are a sinner? Do you know that you have a Saviour? Do you trust in the precious blood of our Lord Jesus Christ? And if she should say, "Yes, I do," I should say, Do you wish to take your place with God's people, and join with them in commemorating our Lord's death? And if she should say "I do," I should say: Come into the church, it may be you will get light on these other questions by and by. Any one whom I have reason to believe Christ would admit into heaven, I would admit to the Lord's table. And, therefore, I would admit to the communion table and receive into the church many whose theological views I could not approve, and who could not subscribe to the Confession of Faith.

We believe, moreover, that the children of believers are also members of the church, and, therefore, it is not strictly correct to speak of them as *joining the church.* They belong to the visible church by virtue of their relation to the household covenant. They are members of the church, and being members, they have a right to the sacraments of the church; to baptism in their infancy, and to the Lord's Supper when they reach a suitable age, "if they be free from scandal, appear sober and steady, and have knowledge to discern the Lord's body." This quotation from our directory for worship is to be followed up however by another which says that those who are admitted to sealing ordinances shall be "examined as to their knowledge and piety."

I have presented in outline the leading characteristics of the Presbyterian system both in polity and doctrine. In addition to what has been said, it is to be noticed that it has these considerations to recommend it; its liberality and its elasticity.

We do not unchurch other denominations, though preferring our own. We do not say that Episcopacy is not a proper form of church government; we do not deny that it has its excellencies. If a Christian community wishes a polity which makes a great deal of three orders in the ministry we have no objection. We recognize the validity of the Episcopal ordination. If men prefer the Congregational mode, sigh for liberty, and cannot be at home in the Presbyterian Church, we say, We do not agree with you in this matter, but have no fault to find. We recognize the validity of Congregational ordination. We do not deny the validity of baptism by immersion, and if a man thinks he would be more effectually baptized in a river than in a basin I should not blame him for applying to a Baptist minister. It is the liberality of the Presbyterian Church, the open door which it offers to all who are Christ's, joined with strict conservatism so far as its office-bearers are concerned, which constitutes in great measure the strength of Presbyterianism.

And the system is elastic. There is room for play of choice within the cardinal principles of Presbyterian polity. The Presbyterian Church and the Reformed Church are near akin — only their catechism is the Heidelburg, ours the Westminster; they have a liturgy, we have none; their ministers wear the Geneva gown which our ministers have laid aside, though some, we see, are putting them on again. The Presbyterian Church and the Methodist Church are closely related, so far as church government is concerned; only their bishop is a sort of perpetual moderator, while our moderator of Presbytery is changed every six months. The Reformed Episcopal Church in discarding the doctrine of apostolic succession, has eliminated the element which keeps Presbyterianism and Episcopacy apart.

I do not know how far you will agree with me in these remarks. If I have presented Presbyterianism in a more liberal aspect than you have been accustomed to regard it, I can only say that the views I have presented can all be verified at your pleasure by referring to our Form of government. If I have removed from the minds of any the impression that ours is a narrow, repressing religion, I shall be glad. If I have said anything to increase your respect or rouse your enthusiasm for our system of doctrine and polity, I shall feel that I have accomplished good. Our church has a history of which we may be proud. The history of Presbyterianism is one of the grandest chapters in the history of civil liberty. To the Presbyterian Church is assigned the high honor of being the earnest advocate and defender of that doctrinal system which magnifies Go(and makes His glory the end of the universe. Our doctrines are true, and ou: polity is scriptural, practical, wise, and consonant with the spirit of republica government. What we need is not a change of creed or polity, but a full appre ciation of the one and a faithful administration of the other. We have machiner which is well adapted to the work we have to do. It is only necessary for u to put it into effective exercise, and go on, in harmony with our brethren of othe Christian names, to the conquest of the world for Jesus.

www.ingramcontent.com/pod-product-compliance
Lightning Source LLC
LaVergne TN
LVHW020635110826
845149LV00004B/1214

* 9 7 8 1 4 1 8 1 9 1 2 3 8 *